MATT CHRISTOPHER

In the Goal with . . .

Briana Scurry

MATT CHRISTOPHER

In the Goal with ...
Briana Scurry

Little, Brown and Company

Boston   New York   London

First Edition

Matt Christopher™ is a trademark of Catherine M. Christopher.

Library of Congress Cataloging-in-Publication Data

Stout, Glenn.
    In the goal with . . . Briana Scurry / Glenn Stout — 1st ed.
       p. cm.
    Summary: A biography of the soccer goalkeeper whose play on the United States National Team earned her the nickname "The Rock."
    ISBN 0-316-13507-0 (pb)
    1. Scurry, Briana, 1971–   — Juvenile literature.   2. Soccer players — United States — Biography — Juvenile literature.
[1. Scurry, Briana, 1971–   .   2. Soccer players.
3. Afro-Americans — Biography.   4. Women — Biography.]
I. Title.
GV942.7.S37 C57   2000
796.334'092 — dc21
[B]   99-087904

10 9 8 7 6 5 4 3 2 1

COM-MO

Printed in the United States of America

Contents

MATT CHRISTOPHER

In the Goal with . . .

Briana Scurry

Chapter One:
1971-1989

The Eye of the Hurricane

Briana Scurry knows pressure.

As goalkeeper for the United States women's national soccer team, Briana is the team's last line of defense. If the opposition somehow manages to steal the ball from Mia Hamm and maneuver it past Brandi Chastain, Julie Foudy, Michelle Akers, and Kate Sobrero, they still have to get it past the player teammates call "The Rock," Briana Scurry.

During the game Briana never takes her eyes off the ball. She constantly looks downfield, following the play. As she does, she paces back and forth across the goalmouth, staying loose, keeping track of every player on the field, remaining ready.

Her teammates sometimes do their jobs so well that the other team can't even get the ball into the American half of the field, much less take a shot on goal. "When my team is down in the other end, I love it," says Briana. She often spends most of the game waiting for something to happen.

But she knows that can change in an instant. In just a few seconds one great pass or a mistake by the defense can create a chance for the opposition to score. Briana has to be ready, barking out instructions to her teammates, cutting down the angle to the goal, and preparing to either jump in the air or dive along the ground to block a shot.

At the moment a shot is taken, she knows that everyone is watching her and that her teammates are depending on her to keep the other team from scoring. She knows that the outcome of the game might be determined by how she performs. Somehow, some way, this five-foot-eight-inch woman has to cover a goal that measures twenty-four feet wide and eight feet high.

Until the shot is actually taken Briana doesn't know what she might have to do. She might have to charge out of the goal toward the shooter and try to catch the shot in her hands. Or she may have to dive sideways through the air and punch the ball away with her fist. She may have to jump up and tip the shot over the crossbar or even slide along the ground and kick it away with her foot. She has to be ready for every possibility.

Briana Scurry welcomes the pressure. "I love knowing that I can control the outcome of a game myself," she says. Her ability to play her best when the pressure is greatest has made her one of the best goalkeepers in the world.

As national team coach Tony DiCicco once told a reporter, "She has a great mind for the game. She never looks panicked. She always looks calm, even when she isn't. That's invaluable for a goalkeeper."

Indeed, no other goalkeeper in the world can surpass her ability to stay calm and focused in high-pressure situations. That might be because she has had to live and perform under scrutiny for much of her life. Hers was the only African-American family in her town and she was one of only a handful of African-Americans in her high school. Very few African-Americans play soccer. Briana has said, "Whichever sport I played, I was pretty much the only black kid on the team . . . I've always been a minority."

Some observers have described her demeanor

during a game as like the calm eye in the center of a hurricane. And oddly enough, if not for a hurricane Briana Scurry might never have started playing soccer.

Before Briana was born, her parents, Earnest and Robbie Scurry, lived in Huntsville, Texas, a low-lying city one hundred and thirty miles from the Gulf of Mexico. In 1960, Hurricane Donna struck the city and destroyed the Scurrys' home.

Although no one in the family was hurt, the Scurrys had several young children and worried about what might happen if another hurricane struck. They decided to move somewhere where they would never have to worry about hurricanes again. They moved twelve hundred miles north, all the way to Minneapolis, Minnesota.

In Minneapolis the family continued to grow. Briana Collette Scurry was born on September 7, 1971, the youngest of three brothers and five sisters.

When Briana was in grade school another disaster struck the family. Their new house had been built on filled land over an old lake. The ground was unstable, and as it settled the house started sinking.

The Scurrys wanted to save their house but it was impossible. They had to move for a second time and found a home in the small farming community of Dayton, about fifteen miles north of Minneapolis.

Dayton was a nice place, but the Scurrys were the only African-American family in town, which sometimes made it uncomfortable for the Scurry children to grow up there. Although their neighbors accepted the Scurrys, it was still hard on the children.

Fortunately Briana's parents and siblings helped her make the adjustment. "I never got singled out," she recalled later. "My parents never let me think I was alone in anything. They taught me I could do whatever I wanted to do."

When Briana was very young, she was shy and not very assertive. One day when she was seven years old she came home and told her mother that another girl had pushed her down. Her parents sensed that their daughter lacked self-confidence. "I wasn't going to let that happen again," her mother said later. She immediately enrolled Briana in a karate class.

Although karate is a martial art, the Scurrys didn't

send Briana to karate class to learn how to fight. The real lesson of the sport is the discipline and self-control it takes to learn karate.

Briana loved going to class. Each week she learned more moves and became a little bit better, which made her feel good about herself. She didn't use her skills to fight, but learning karate gave her self-confidence. She eventually became proficient enough to earn a brown belt, only one level short of the sport's highest achievement, a black belt.

She enjoyed being with the other students and discovered that playing sports was a way to make friends. She learned that differences of race didn't matter to her teammates.

The local youth association sponsored many different sports leagues. They passed out flyers at Briana's grade school, so kids could sign up for sports. Each time Briana received a flyer she raced home after school and begged her parents to let her play. "You get a flyer, take it home, and for fifteen bucks you get to play a sport," she later told a reporter.

Briana was soon playing nearly every sport the youth association offered: football, floor hockey, baseball, basketball, track — and soccer. Playing sports became her favorite way to spend her spare time. Her mother recalled later, "You didn't insult her with a doll."

When Briana was ten years old, she signed up to play soccer in nearby Brooklyn Park. But when she went to her first practice, she got a big surprise.

All of her teammates were boys!

Briana wasn't aware of it, but she was a pioneer. Women had been playing soccer in the United States for only a few years. In fact, just twenty years earlier the notion of women playing soccer — or almost any other sport — would have been nearly unthinkable.

Until the early 1970s, opportunities for women and girls to play sports were few. Apart from track and field, ice skating, gymnastics, and a few other sports, not many women even tried to play sports. Most people thought women lacked the strength and stamina to play.

But in the early 1970s, women began to demand equal rights on the playing field. Given the chance to compete, a new generation of female athletes proved that women had the same capacity to play sports as men.

Briana didn't know any of this when she signed up for soccer. She just knew that she wanted to play.

She didn't know much about soccer, but neither did many of her teammates. Unlike baseball, football, or basketball, soccer wasn't on television very often and there was no major professional league to follow.

But soccer was beginning to become more popular, particularly with kids. Players didn't need a whole lot of equipment or special skills. They just needed to be able to run. Parents thought the game was safer than other sports and encouraged their children to play. Youth soccer leagues were growing rapidly.

At Briana's first practice, the coaches tried to instruct the players on the fundamentals of the game, such as how to kick the ball with either foot, how to dribble, and how to make a header. One of Briana's coaches played goalkeeper, blocking the shots of the players. Then he asked if any of the kids wanted to play goalkeeper.

None of the boys stepped forward. They were afraid they might get hurt trying to block the ball.

But Briana wasn't afraid. She jumped right in the

goal. She joked later, "I liked it because I liked flopping around on the ground."

Ever so slowly, Briana began to learn the special techniques of a goalkeeper. At first, she wasn't quite sure what to do, and tried to catch every shot with her hands. But her coaches explained that it really didn't matter how she stopped a shot, as long as she stopped it. They taught her to jump up for high shots to knock them over the goal, and to dive for shots to either side to knock them wide with both hands. They told her to keep her eyes on the ball and to try to anticipate what was going to happen next.

Although she eventually shared the position with another player, and sometimes played in the field because her coaches wanted everyone on the team to know how to play a complete game, Briana liked playing goalkeeper the best. Even though she sometimes didn't touch the ball for a long time, playing goalkeeper made her feel important. "As a goalkeeper, if the other team is going to win, it has to get by you first," she has said.

But soccer wasn't the only sport Briana wanted to play. When she was eleven, the youth association passed out flyers for a tackle football league. Briana signed up. She was a fast runner for her age, and very well coordinated. Even though she was one of only a few girls in the league, she wasn't intimidated. She loved the fact that she could "hit people and not get into trouble," as she said later. She was one of the best players on her team. She played cornerback and wide receiver and scored nine touchdowns during the season. But when she had to move up to another weight division, her mother decided that it was time for Briana to give up football.

Briana's interest in sports continued to grow. When she wasn't playing, she was watching sports on television. When she watched the 1984 Summer Olympics and saw American medalists like gymnast Mary Lou Retton and track star Jackie Joyner-Kersee, she told her parents that she was going to be in the Olympics someday. They didn't laugh at her or tell her she was silly. Instead, they encouraged her. Her mother later recalled, "When Briana sets her mind on something, she becomes very determined. When someone says she can't do something, she will work extra hard to prove that she can. I didn't doubt it for a minute when she talked of being in the Olympics someday."

By the time Briana entered junior high school, she had two dreams. One was to be a track star. The other was to become a lawyer. For as much as she loved sports, she also loved learning.

But as Briana started to grow up, the girl who was faster than everyone else suddenly had some competition. When kids go through puberty their bodies mature and change. Sometimes the kids who were the best athletes suddenly became awkward. That didn't happen to Briana, but she still had to make some adjustments. As she recalled later, "everyone got faster" in junior high. But that didn't stop Briana. She just changed dreams.

Winters are long and cold in Minnesota, making it almost impossible to play soccer or run track. So in the winter Briana turned her attention to basketball. Although she continued to play other sports, basketball soon became her favorite.

Briana was only five foot eight, not very tall for a basketball player, but she was tough. She played power forward and usually led her team in rebounds. She was one of the best players of her age in metropolitan Minneapolis. But because she couldn't play basketball all year long, in the summer she started playing soccer for a club team known as the Strikers, to stay in shape.

She played soccer in high school, too, making the varsity team as a freshman at Anoka Regional High School and even being named to the all-conference team. But Briana never thought soccer, or any of the other sports that she played, would be important to her future.

As it turned out, the fact that she played so many different sports helped give her a great advantage in soccer. Basketball helped with her footwork and speed, running track gave her endurance, and softball and karate helped her hand-eye coordination and quickness.

Playing goalkeeper was the one activity that allowed her to use all of her skills. Few other goalkeepers could match her all-around athleticism. On occasion, her coaches even moved her from goalkeeper and played her at other positions to take advantage of her speed. And when her team was involved in an overtime round of penalty kicks, Briana often kicked in addition to playing goal.

At Anoka High, Briana played soccer, basketball, and softball and ran track. And every year she got a little better, eventually lettering in all four sports. In both her sophomore and junior years, Briana was named to the all-state team in soccer, and won all-conference honors in track by helping her team to a fourth-place finish in the state meet in both the 400- and 800-meter relays. She also competed in the long jump and finished second in the state in the 100-meter dash. For all her talents on the field and in the classroom, she was named an Academic All-American.

People were beginning to realize that Briana was something special.

Chapter Two:

1989-1990

Tough Decision for a Tornado

In the summer of 1989, before her senior year of high school, Briana was playing with her club team, the Strikers. The team was made up of many of the best female soccer players in the state. The year before they had won the state championship.

Coach Pete Swenson expected more from the team in 1989. With Briana in the goal they swept to another state title and took aim on the national championship.

Briana liked soccer, but she still thought her future was in basketball. She hoped to earn a scholarship to play in college. She was a very good basketball player, but at only five foot eight, she wasn't quite big enough to play forward at a Division One school. But many smaller, Division Two schools were beginning to recruit her.

But Briana's life began to change as the Strikers played in the national tournament. In the regional semifinals, Briana led her team to a win almost by herself.

The opposing team from Kansas mounted a relentless attack, and the Strikers' defense broke down. All of a sudden Briana was alone in the net with a half dozen players in front of her all trying to score. Another player might have panicked, but this was the kind of situation Briana loved.

Someone shot a low line drive to her side. Briana dove and blocked the ball back out with her hands. As she scrambled back to her feet another Kansas player sent the ball rocketing toward the goal. Once more Briana dove and blocked the shot.

But her Striker teammates still couldn't clear the ball. Briana got back onto her feet just as another Kansas player sent a shot toward the upper corner of the net. Briana jumped like she was going up to block a shot in basketball. She punched the ball free and this time her teammates were able to clear it away.

In twelve seconds Briana had made a remarkable three saves! Coach Swenson later said, "When I saw that, I realized she could do anything." The Strikers won. Although they lost their next game, in the regional finals, Briana's standout play in the goal was the talk of the tournament.

Swenson told Briana that she might want to reconsider playing basketball in college. He told her that she might get a better offer from a Division One school to play soccer. Briana was surprised, but intrigued. Although basketball was still her favorite sport, she started her senior year at Anoka High determined to find out just how good a soccer player she could be. Briana had been named to the all-state team as a junior and she hoped to repeat as a senior.

But the performance of her team was more important than her own individual accomplishments. Although the Anoka Tornadoes had a good record in 1988, even with Briana in the goal they hadn't been considered one of the elite teams in the state. But in 1989, they were a senior-laden team, and Briana hoped to help her teammates end their high school careers with a state title.

Unfortunately, at the beginning of the year some of the Tornadoes weren't focused on their goal. Three starting players missed some practices.

That was a violation of team rules. Coach Dave

Tank knew that something had to be done. But he didn't discipline players himself. He left those decisions to the two team captains. They decided that the three players who missed the practices would have to sit out the first two games of the season.

Anoka lost both games. But when the three suspended players returned to the team, the Tornadoes started to come together.

Then Coach Tank made a small change in the lineup. Thus far the Anoka defense simply hadn't been playing very well. They weren't giving Briana any help. As good as she was, she didn't stand much of a chance when the opposition was constantly on the attack.

Coach Tank moved one of the Tornadoes' best players, Shannon Jaakola, from offense to defense. The team immediately began to play better.

Still, after their two early-season losses, no one gave the Tornadoes much of a chance. In early October they played back-to-back games against Blaine, ranked number five in the state, and Roseville, ranked number nine. To make the state tournament, unranked Anoka would have to beat both schools.

17

Briana came up big. The Anoka defense played tight in both games and neither opponent was able to get a shot past Briana. Anoka tied Blaine, 0–0, and beat Roseville, 3–0.

Briana's performance gave her team a lift. Over the next three weeks, Briana led them to three more wins, giving up only one goal. Out of nowhere, Anoka qualified for the state tournament.

In the tournament, Briana and her teammates played even better. They dumped St. Francis, 7–0, and Coon Rapids, 3–0, to win their section. Then Briana recorded her eleventh shutout of the season and remarkable seventh in a row as Anoka beat Stillwater, 1–0, in the quarterfinals.

They faced tough St. Paul Academy in the semifinals at the Metrodome, the huge enclosed stadium in Minneapolis where the Minnesota Vikings play football. Few observers thought Anoka had a chance.

But Briana's presence in the goal gave her teammates confidence. Knowing that she was behind them, ready to keep the ball out of the net, they weren't afraid to play aggressively.

Anoka jumped out to a quick 1–0 lead to put the

pressure on St. Paul. Shannon Jaakola keyed a tough defense that prevented St. Paul from even taking a shot during the first half. In the second, the Tornadoes increased their lead to 3–0 before St. Paul was finally able to mount an attack and score a goal in the last minute of the game. But it was too little, too late. Anoka won, 3–1, to reach the finals against powerhouse Park.

Anoka's defense came through again. In the first half they stopped Park cold. Unfortunately, Park was also able to stop Anoka.

In the second half Park threatened to break through. Two expert headers off a throw-in sent the ball all the way across the goalmouth to a player waiting patiently at the edge of the penalty area.

Any other goalkeeper would have been fooled. But Briana calmly tracked each pass. When the Park player took her shot, Briana was in perfect position and stopped it. A few minutes later she blocked a twenty-yard kick.

But Anoka was no more successful against Park's defense. Regulation time ended in a 0–0 tie. The championship would be decided by a shoot-out.

In a shoot-out each team selects five players to

alternate taking shots from the penalty mark, twelve yards from the goal. Whichever team scores the most goals in the shoot-out wins the game.

A shoot-out is one of the most pressure-packed moments in sports, particularly for the goalkeeper, who must remain in place in the center of the goal until the ball is kicked, then try to block or deflect it out of the goal. That is incredibly difficult because it is impossible for the goalkeeper to cover the entire twenty-four-foot width of the goal. It is particularly difficult for female goalies for the simple reason that they are usually smaller than the men for whom the goal dimensions were designed. If the shooter makes a hard, accurate kick just inside the post, the goalkeeper doesn't have a chance to block the shot, even if she correctly guesses where it is going.

But the goalkeeper isn't completely powerless. As the keeper stands before the net, she can try to psyche the opponent out by staring her down, or try to anticipate which way the kick is going by analyzing the way the shooter approaches the ball.

Anoka was actually pleased when the game went to a shoot-out. In the weeks before the game they'd spent hours practicing shoot-outs, and besides, they had Briana Scurry in their goal.

Anoka shot first and missed. Then it was Park's turn. The Park player approached the ball. Briana crouched before the net.

Although the goalkeeper may not move her feet before the ball is shot, she is allowed to shift her body. As the shooter approached the ball Briana put on her game face, looked her in the eye, and swayed back and forth menacingly. She revealed after the game, "I learned that [swaying back and forth] this summer at a tournament. It makes the shooter think you can cover more territory than you really can, and sometimes makes them miss."

The Park player shot and it went wide of the net! Briana's strategy had worked!

But the second Anoka player missed her shot as well. Once again a Park player approached the ball. Amazingly, it, too, went wide.

With Anoka's third shot, Shannon Jaakola put the team ahead, 1–0. Briana stuffed the next Park shot to keep Anoka in the lead.

Now it was Briana's turn to kick. She left her goal and jogged slowly to the other end of the field. She paused before the ball, took a few quick steps, and drilled it past the Park goalkeeper. Now Anoka led, 2–0!

The next Park player finally got the ball past Briana, but when Anoka's fifth shooter blasted her shot past the goalmouth, the Tornadoes' lead was insurmountable. Anoka won, 3–1.

After the game Coach Tank said, "As long as we've got Briana Scurry, we'll take a shoot-out every time. When I was coaching the boys' soccer team a few years ago, we had an All-American goalkeeper. I would say Briana is right up there with him."

Reporters crowded around Briana after the game. They had been surprised when Briana took the penalty kick. She explained, "The goalkeeper knows exactly how hard it is for another goalkeeper to stop a penalty kick." One reporter wrote, "If there had been a most valuable player award, Scurry would have gotten it."

She had ended her high school career with a goals against average (GAA) of only 0.94. To no one's surprise, a few days later Briana earned her third straight all-state selection. She was also named a second-team All-American.

Briana had done what she'd set out to do — end her high school soccer career on a high note. But as she began preparing for her final year of basketball, Briana realized that she had to start looking toward her future. More than seventy colleges were recruiting her to play sports. Some wanted her just to play basketball, some wanted her just to run track, and some wanted her just to play soccer. A few wanted her to participate in all three!

Briana had some decisions to make.

Chapter Three:
1990–1991

The Minutewoman

Briana Scurry was fortunate to have so many options. Only a few years earlier, it would have been almost impossible for a female athlete to earn an athletic scholarship to college. Most colleges sponsored only a few women's teams and scholarships were rare.

But in 1971, the United States federal government enacted a regulation known as Title IX, which forbids any school that receives federal funds to discriminate on the basis of sex. Over the next decade a series of legal challenges resulted in court decisions ruling that Title IX applies to athletic programs. This means that schools have to provide the same opportunities for female athletes as they do for male athletes.

As a result, women's athletic programs in both

colleges and high schools expanded rapidly, and colleges began giving more athletic scholarships to women.

Due to Title IX, women's soccer grew rapidly. In 1982, the National Collegiate Athletic Association (NCAA), the organization that controls college sports, held the first national women's collegiate soccer tournament. Every year more and more schools added women's soccer programs, particularly on the East and West Coasts, where men's soccer was an established sport. (In the Midwest, only a few schools played high-level soccer.) Talented players with good academic records, like Briana, were in demand.

Pete Swenson, Briana's coach with the Strikers, thought she had tremendous potential. Very few goalkeepers in women's soccer were as athletic as Briana. He wanted to make sure she went to a good school with a good soccer program.

He contacted an old friend named Jim Rudy, who had just been named soccer coach at the University of Massachusetts. He told Rudy that he knew of a player whom he thought could help a college program win a lot of games.

Rudy decided to travel to Minnesota to see Briana play. He was immediately impressed. She had the quickest hands and feet he had ever seen.

And he was even more impressed by Briana's attitude and composure. "Even if she was rattled, I couldn't see it," he told a reporter years later. "That's a great place to start with a goalkeeper. Most keepers, if there's a mistake, they show it to their teammates, which is bad. Even worse, they show it to the other team." But Briana kept her cool.

Though the UMass women's soccer team was on the rise and coming off an appearance in the NCAA tournament, Rudy was still building the UMass program. He knew he would need a goalkeeper who could keep her cool. She would probably be facing a lot of shots. Rudy made up his mind and offered Briana a soccer scholarship.

At first, Briana was hesitant. She wasn't certain soccer was what she wanted to play in college. As much as she liked soccer, she still liked basketball more.

But Briana was also realistic. She said later, "I was All-American in soccer, I was all-state in basketball." She visited the UMass campus and knew she would feel comfortable there. Finally, she decided to accept Rudy's scholarship offer.

But before Briana went off to UMass she still had to complete her senior year at Anoka. She turned her attention to basketball and led the Tornadoes to one of their most successful seasons ever, earning all-conference, all-metro, and all-state honors.

"Despite not being tall, she can play inside," coach Jeff Leslie said of Scurry, who led the team in both rebounding and scoring. "When the game was on the line, we went to her; she wanted the ball." At the end of the school year she was named the top female athlete in Minnesota.

The awards were nice, but Briana knew that once she made it to UMass, they wouldn't mean anything. The UMass Minutewomen played a rigorous schedule, and she was certain to be challenged like never before — on the field and off.

Briana Scurry was, and still is, something of a rarity in women's soccer. Very few African-Americans play soccer.

"Soccer's not a sport that's in the inner city at all," she once explained, pointing out that many African-Americans live in the inner city. "There's no place to play," she went on. "You go in the inner city and what do you see? Tar. And what do you play on tar? Basketball. It [soccer] is just not something kids are exposed to." In all of the inner-city areas of Minneapolis, for example, there was only one soccer field.

For this reason, the American Youth Soccer Organization (AYSO), which operates most youth soccer leagues, is most active in suburban areas. Since few African-Americans live in those areas, they don't get the same exposure to soccer that suburban kids do. Also, African-American kids tend to identify with African-American athletes, just as Latino kids identify with Latino players and white kids identify with white players. Since there are so few African-American soccer players, kids don't have role models to follow. One soccer official has commented, "We have to sell African-Americans on the sport. There are not enough African-Americans playing the game."

The University of Massachusetts is in Amherst, in the western part of the state in the foothills of the Berkshire Mountains. It is a big state university of almost twenty thousand students. Yet even at a large school like UMass, there were relatively few

African-Americans. But she was accustomed to being the only African-American on her team, once describing her experience on the soccer field as like that of a "fly in the milk."

Briana quickly discovered that college was much different from high school, both in the classroom and socially. Students came to the school from all over the country. The schoolwork was much harder than in high school, and she also had to spend several hours each day at soccer practice. The collegiate soccer season takes place in the fall, so as soon as Briana arrived at UMass she began playing soccer. She had never been so busy in her entire life.

Although Briana had been a dominant goalkeeper in high school, collegiate soccer was a different game. Most high school teams had only a few talented players. Many players had limited skills and it had been easy for Briana to block their shots. Her entire game was based on her instincts and athletic ability. In high school she had never worried much about the more technical aspects of goalkeeping, like footwork and positioning. Scurry later said, "When I came in [to college] I was very short on the tactical and technical aspects of goalkeeping."

Coach Rudy immediately began working with her. He was one of the most experienced coaches in women's soccer. Before coming to UMass, he had been women's soccer coach at Central Florida, where he coached Michelle Akers, who many observers believed to be the greatest female soccer player in the world.

Scurry was one of the most gifted players he had coached since Akers. He worked with her at practice for hours, trying to teach her what she needed to know to play collegiate soccer.

In high school, like most other goalkeepers, she had stayed close to the goal line. She had been fast enough to simply move back and forth right in front of the goal to stop shots. That approach wouldn't work in college. Almost every player she faced was faster and more talented than anyone she had played against in high school. Teams knew how to play together and pass the ball to get it into the best position. Athletic ability and instinct wouldn't be enough.

For the first time she actually had to study the game. She had to learn to anticipate what the opposition was likely to do in various situations. She had to learn when to stay in the net and allow play to come to her, and when to come out from the goal and cut down the shooter's angle. She also had to learn to help direct her team's defense. In effect, she had to learn how to play goalkeeper in an entirely new way.

And for the first time ever, Briana Scurry wasn't necessarily the best goalkeeper on her team. Rudy already had a great goalkeeper, Skye Eddy. He planned to alternate Eddy and Scurry in the net. But when Eddy was playing goalkeeper, he still wanted to take advantage of Scurry's talents.

Rudy had seen during practices that Scurry was one of the fastest players on the team. For the first time in years she was asked to play in the field, at forward. Despite having hardly ever played the position before, Briana more than held her own.

Playing in the field helped her understanding of the game when she returned to the net. That was good, for while Scurry didn't mind sharing duties at goalkeeper, eventually she wanted the job for herself.

Splitting time with Eddy, Briana played ten games in goal during her freshman year. Although she recorded three shutouts, she was inconsistent and occasionally gave up easy goals after making spectacular saves. In fact, inconsistency was a problem for the team. The Minutewomen were young and inexperienced. They finished the season with a so-so record.

At the end of her freshman year she didn't return to Minnesota to live. Instead, she stayed in Massachusetts and played on a club team in Boston, honing her skills for her sophomore season. It was a good thing she did, for when practice began in the fall, Skye Eddy got hurt. Rather than risk further injury, Eddy decided to sit out, or "redshirt," the season and return in 1992. Scurry became the starting goalkeeper for the Minutewomen.

She responded in spectacular fashion. In nineteen games she gave up only nine goals and had a remarkable twelve shutouts.

Near the end of the 1991 season, Coach Rudy told Briana that he thought she was good enough to play for the United States national team. Scurry said, "What's that?" He explained to her that the U.S. women's national team was made up of the best female soccer players in the United States. They played other national teams from around the world and were World Cup champions. Briana didn't even know there was a Women's World Cup.

Rudy told Scurry that he thought she had the ability to play at that level. In fact, he had already spoken to national team coach Anson Dorrance, telling him, "I might have your next national team goalkeeper."

Briana was stunned. Although she had been successful, she didn't consider herself one of the best goalkeepers in the country. There were times when she felt she really didn't know what she was doing, that she was just getting by on instinct and luck. She knew she wasn't working as hard as she could to be the best she could be.

The U.S. women's national team had been created in 1985. Under Coach Dorrance, who also served as women's soccer coach at the University of North Carolina, the American squad had captured the first Women's World Cup, held in China in 1991, by defeating Norway, 2–1.

The more Scurry learned about the national team, the more she wanted to play on it. She started taking soccer more seriously.

She wasn't the only one who was giving women's soccer more attention. The United States Olympic Committee (USOC) was also taking a long, hard look at the sport. Women's soccer was not yet an Olympic sport, but the USOC was certain that someday it would be. They wanted to make sure the United States was prepared to compete. To that end, in 1992 they included women's soccer in the United States Olympic Festival, a big sports competition designed to help the American Olympic effort.

As one of the top collegiate goalkeepers in the country, Scurry was selected to participate in the festival, playing for a regional team that would compete against the national team. Coach Dorrance attended the tournament to scout players. He hadn't forgotten what Coach Rudy had told him about Briana. Before her first game, he came over to her and said, "I'll be watching you."

When he said that, Briana suddenly got nervous. She had a hard time focusing on the game. Instead of concentrating on what she was supposed to do, she was distracted by thoughts of what would happen if she didn't play well.

She ended up playing one of the worst games of her life. She gave up three goals in only fifteen minutes and was replaced at halftime.

Briana was disappointed in herself. She had let the pressure get to her and was certain she had blown her chance to ever make the national team.

But Dorrance didn't feel that way. He knew it wasn't fair to judge her solely on her performance in the tournament. After all, she had never played with most of her teammates, and there were some defensive breakdowns. The goals weren't all Scurry's fault.

And even though she had allowed three goals, she had also made some remarkable saves. She was so fast and quick that she didn't have to dive as often as most other goalkeepers. That's a real advantage, because if a goalkeeper can stay on her feet she has a much better chance of stopping rebounds than a goalkeeper who is lying on the ground.

Briana didn't know it, but Dorrance had been impressed with her skills and athleticism despite her performance. He didn't view her as a failure. Instead, he saw a player with tremendous potential who was still learning how to play the game. Dorrance was already thinking ahead to the next

Women's World Cup, as well as the Olympics. And it just so happened that veteran national team goalkeeper Mary Harvey had a torn ligament in her knee. Dorrance knew that he would likely need to replace her soon. He thought Briana Scurry might be that replacement.

At the end of the summer Scurry was excited to be one of about sixty players invited to attend a ten-day training camp with the national team at Babson College, outside Boston. She thought it would be her last chance to make an impression on Dorrance and his goalkeeper coach, Tony DiCicco, who had yet to see her play in person.

In addition to working on various drills, the players were split into four teams that scrimmaged nearly every day. This gave the coaches a chance to watch the players under a variety of conditions and with a variety of teammates.

This time Briana didn't let the pressure get to her. She stayed focused. DiCicco later recalled, "She didn't play all that well [but] her great qualities were embedded in my mind," including what DiCicco described as "explosive athletic skills." She was one of the few players not already on the national team to impress the two coaches. Although she wasn't immediately put on the team, Dorrance told her she had done well and said later, "We earmarked her for the future."

As Briana would soon learn, her future would include a lot more soccer.

Chapter Four:
1992–1994

Super Seasons

After training camp Scurry returned to UMass, ready to begin the 1992 soccer season. The Minute-women hoped to build on the 1991 season and looked forward to making it to the NCAA tournament.

But coach Jim Rudy faced a quandary. Skye Eddy was healthy again and ready to play in the goal. Despite Scurry's great 1991 season, Rudy resumed alternating the two players in goal. Although neither player was particularly happy about the arrangement, they couldn't argue with the results.

UMass surged out of the blocks to open the season 10–0, gaining the number-five ranking in the country. Skye Eddy was the leading goalkeeper in the nation.

But in the final weeks of the season, UMass stumbled, losing three of their final eight games and finishing the season ranked tenth in the country with a record of 15–3. Despite their late-season struggles, they were one of twelve teams selected for the NCAA tournament.

Even though Skye Eddy finished the regular season with a GAA of 0.64, fifth-best in the nation, Coach Rudy decided to use Scurry in the goal for the first tournament game, against Connecticut.

Briana did not disappoint. She made several spectacular saves, and the game went scoreless in the first half. But in the second half, a low shot ricocheted off a UMass defender and trickled past Scurry for a goal. UMass trailed, 1–0.

The Minutewomen appeared to be on their way to defeat. But with only eight minutes remaining a Connecticut Husky player punched a header out of the goal with her hand.

The referee immediately blew the whistle and held up a red card. UMass would get to take a penalty kick. Briana's teammate Kim Eynard lined up the shot and knocked it in to tie the game, 1–1.

A few minutes later, the game ended. Since the score was tied, the two teams played a fifteen-minute overtime period. Neither squad was able to score, so they played a second fifteen-minute overtime. While Scurry held steady, her teammates finally broke through the UConn defense to score. UMass won, 2–1, to advance to the second round of the tournament.

Their opponent was the University of Hartford, one of the three teams they had lost to in the regular season. At the start of the game, UMass seemed determined to pay Hartford back for that defeat. Through tough, focused play and strong defense, they scored first, then nursed their 1–0 lead into the second half. But then their defense made a mistake. After Scurry made a spectacular save the defense failed to clear the ball, and Hartford tied the game.

The score seemed to unnerve the Minutewomen. A few minutes later UMass committed a foul and the referee awarded Hartford an indirect kick. The play fooled Briana; Hartford scored to take a 2–1 lead and went on to win the game.

Scurry was disappointed with the defeat but she knew she'd tried her best. Still, she was determined to get even better.

In the off-season she worked out harder than ever

before. She even lifted weights, something very few female athletes were doing at the time. When she reported back to the team in the fall of 1993, she had added ten pounds of muscle. "I started getting to balls I'd never gotten to before," Briana recalls. She set a personal goal to beat out Skye Eddy for the starting position.

As the beginning of the season approached, it became obvious to everyone on the team that Briana would achieve her goal. Although Eddy was playing well, Scurry had improved dramatically.

A week before the season started, Eddy abruptly left school, transferring to George Mason University. Now Scurry was the team's first-string goalkeeper.

She quickly proved that her preseason performance hadn't been a fluke. Led by her remarkable goalkeeping, the Minutewomen finished the regular season with a record of 15–2–3, winning the Atlantic 10 Conference for the second year in a row. Despite playing in seven overtime contests, Scurry gave up only six goals during the regular season. She led the nation's goalkeepers with a minuscule GAA of only 0.36.

The Minutewomen easily qualified for the NCAA

tournament. In the Northeast Regional Semifinals, they dumped Providence, 5–0, to set up a rematch with UConn. The winner would advance to the Final Four.

The game was a tough defensive battle played out at midfield. Neither team had many chances to score until, with thirty minutes remaining in the game, UMass forward Rachel Leduc outraced the Connecticut goalkeeper for a loose ball and poked it into the net to give UMass a 1–0 lead. If Scurry could hold the Huskies scoreless, UMass would make the Final Four and have a chance to win the national championship.

UConn tried everything to score a goal to tie the game, but the UMass defense gave them few opportunities to shoot. And when they did get a shot off, they couldn't get the ball past Briana. UMass won, 1–0. After the game Briana and her teammates were ecstatic. "It has been a long time coming," Briana said. "It's a dream come true for me to get to the Final Four."

But that dream meant that UMass would have to play number-one North Carolina in the national semifinals. Anson Dorrance's Tar Heels were easily the best women's collegiate soccer team in the nation. They had won seven consecutive NCAA titles.

Their roster was a virtual all-star team that included several players, like scoring sensation Mia Hamm and midfielder Tisha Venturini, who also played for Dorrance on the national team. No other team in women's collegiate soccer could match the Tar Heels' combination of talent and experience. In order to win, every player on the UMass team would have to play the best game of her life.

The Tar Heels got off to a quick start and put the pressure on UMass. Only eleven minutes into the game, Mia Hamm was fouled in the box. She converted her penalty kick against Scurry to put North Carolina ahead, 1–0.

With a lead, North Carolina could afford to take even more chances on offense. Under relentless pressure, the UMass defense began to break up. Time and time again the Tar Heels attacked the goal. Scurry played well, but by halftime North Carolina had scored twice more to lead, 3–0.

The Minutewomen regrouped at halftime and played better, particularly on defense, but in soccer a 3–0 lead is almost insurmountable. UMass lost,

4–1, as the Minutewomen were able to get off only three shots on goal for the entire game. North Carolina, meanwhile, peppered Scurry with eighteen shots. She made ten saves, including four in the second half that the press described as "spectacular."

After the game, North Carolina coach Anson Dorrance went out of his way to praise Briana. "The goals we scored were a result of our organization in the box," he said. "Scurry is brilliant, but we didn't give her a chance to be brilliant, by moving the ball around her."

Although her collegiate career was over and Briana was disappointed in the loss, she knew she hadn't played her last game of soccer.

Anson Dorrance had invited her to train with the national team.

Chapter Five:
1994–1995

The National Team

Scurry was both thrilled and nervous about the prospect of playing with the national team. Although she'd impressed Coach Dorrance and team goalkeeper coach Tony DiCicco the previous summer, she knew she would have to play much better at training camp in order to make the team.

It was an exciting time to be a soccer player in the United States. In September of 1993, the International Olympic Committee announced that women's soccer would be a medal sport at the 1996 Summer Olympics in Atlanta. And in 1994, the United States would host the Men's World Cup. The combination of those two events promised to raise the profile of both men's and women's soccer throughout the country.

Thus far, the U.S. women's national team had

played and practiced in virtual anonymity. But all of a sudden the team was getting much more attention. Corporations realized that the 1991 World Cup–winning U.S. squad would be favored to win a medal in Atlanta and they began to offer their financial support.

In turn, the United States Soccer Federation (USSF), the organization that runs soccer in the United States, started to treat the team almost as well as the more established men's team. They made plans to build the women's team their own training center in Florida and agreed to start paying team members a small salary. Previously, players on the women's team hadn't received any pay except for room, board, and a small stipend while they trained or traveled with the team. Financial concerns had made it impossible for some players to join the team and had forced others to decide between their financial security and their love of soccer. Being paid made it much easier for many members of the team to keep playing soccer. Now players could train and play soccer on an almost full-time basis. As a result, the team was bound to get better.

Scurry's opportunity to make the team came at a

perfect time for her. Her collegiate soccer career was over and she was in her final year of college. A political science major, she had been considering a career in corporate law and had been planning to apply to law school after graduation. But she put those plans on hold to attend training camp.

She knew she'd have to work hard at camp to make the team. Incumbent goalkeeper Mary Harvey had been on the team since 1986 and was considered one of the best women's goalkeepers in the world. In the 1991 World Cup she had recorded three shutouts. Even though she had missed most of the 1993 season with a knee injury, she was still expected to make the team.

Harvey's injury had given two other goalkeepers a chance to play for the team in 1993, and both had made the most of that opportunity. As Harvey was recuperating, both Jen Mead and Saskia Webber had played impressively. All three goalkeepers were ahead of Scurry when she went to camp. Her chances of making the team seemed slim.

On a good defensive team like the U.S. national team, it sometimes appears as if the goalkeepers have little to do during a game. That impression is misleading, because even though the goalkeeper isn't constantly running like the other players on the field, she has to stay focused.

But anyone who has ever watched a soccer practice would never accuse the goalkeeper of having it easy. In training, goalkeepers are probably the hardest working members of the team. They face hundreds of shots as the various position players, known collectively as outfielders, work on such plays as corner kicks, direct kicks, and penalty shots, and practice shooting on goal.

Although Briana lacked the international experience of Harvey, Mead, and Webber, over the course of camp it became obvious that she was the best athlete of the four. She was simply faster, more mobile, and in better shape.

But athletic ability alone is never enough to succeed in sports. In any kind of sport, physical ability must be combined with experience, determination, and a thorough understanding of the game in order to succeed. Every team has great athletes. The difference between winning and losing often comes down to the mental aspects of the game.

For a goalkeeper, positioning is just as important

as athletic skill. A goalkeeper must understand the game well enough to make the right decision about whether to come out and challenge for a ball, and to guess which of a multitude of players is most likely to take a shot.

This part of Scurry's game needed more work. During camp Coach DiCicco worked closely with her to improve her mental approach. He wanted to see if she could live up to the potential he had seen in her. His reason was simple: Soccer teams that switch back and forth between goalies are rarely successful at the international level. Goalkeeper Mary Harvey's knee was still bothering her, so the U.S. needed to decide upon a new number-one goalkeeper. The team had been invited to participate in the inaugural Algarve Cup, a tournament featuring Europe's best teams, to be held in Portugal in March. They wanted to pick a goalkeeper by then — a goalkeeper they could stick with. DiCicco didn't want to have to worry about who was going to play goal when the team began preparing for the 1995 World Cup.

Scurry made the team as the number-four goalkeeper. She was thrilled, but it was also a bittersweet situation. In order to play with the team she'd have to temporarily withdraw from UMass. She was only a few credits shy of receiving her degree and knew she'd miss all her friends. But she also knew she couldn't pass up the opportunity to join the team. She was in great shape and had just come off the best season of her career. She might never have another opportunity to try out for the team.

For the next few months she trained with the team and continued to work hard. Her play improved dramatically. She soaked up everything Coach DiCicco taught her and impressed everyone with her athleticism, decision making, and leadership skills.

In just a few short months she vaulted past the other three goalkeepers on the team. Coaches Dorrance and DiCicco selected her to play in the Algarve Cup as the team's number-one goalkeeper.

In March of 1994, she traveled with the team to Portugal for the tournament. In the first game, against the Portuguese national team, Scurry started in the American goal.

The game provided a perfect start to Briana's career with the U.S. national team. The Portuguese team played hard, but they were outclassed by the Americans. The U.S. offense scored five goals and their defense was able to shut down Portugal's attacks. On the few occasions they didn't, Scurry was ready. The U.S. won, 5–0. Scurry got a shutout in her first game.

Two days later Scurry recorded another shutout against Sweden. In the last game of the tournament, the U.S. faced Norway. At that time, the rivalry between Norway and the United States was the greatest in women's soccer. The U.S. had been considered fortunate to defeat the more experienced Norwegian team in the inaugural Women's World Cup in 1991. Norway had beaten the Americans twice since and many observers were already looking forward to a rematch between the two clubs in the 1995 World Cup. A matchup between the two squads in the Algarve Cup would provide a good test for both teams. When they played each other it was always a tough, hard-fought game.

This time was no different. Though the U.S. played as hard as they could, Norway once again came away with the victory, 1–0. The game was a big test for Scurry, a test that she passed with flying colors despite the team's defeat. She played well and impressed both her teammates and her coaches. With a combination of athleticism, carefully honed skills, and a cool head, she secured her position in the starting lineup.

A few months later she was tested again in the Chiquita Cup, a tournament held in the United States that featured some of the best women's soccer teams in the world, including Germany, China, and Norway. The tournament would give the Americans a good idea of how well prepared they were to play in the World Cup.

In the first round the United States met Germany at George Mason University, in Fairfax, Virginia, before a crowd of nearly 6,000 fans. At the time, it was one of the largest crowds ever to watch the team play. Scurry said later, "I was a bit nervous; I had never played in front of that many people before."

But if Scurry was nervous, her play didn't show it. She stayed focused the entire game.

Midway through the first half, star German forward Maren Meinart dashed into the open on a breakaway. She raced downfield with the ball all alone. No U.S. defender was within twenty yards of her. Briana Scurry was the only player between Meinart and a goal.

As Meinart approached the net, Scurry tried to read the play and anticipate what the German would do next. This was precisely the part of her game she and Coach DiCicco had worked so long and hard on.

Scurry knew Meinart had no one to pass the ball to and was certain to charge toward the goal. But she also knew that if she stayed back on the goal line, Meinart would have an advantage similar to that of a shooter on a penalty kick.

The only way for Scurry to take away that advantage would be to come out from the goal and challenge Meinart. By doing so, she hoped to cut down on Meinart's angle and give her a smaller portion of the goal to shoot at. Without a moment's hesitation, Scurry dashed fifteen yards out from the goal and crouched down, poised to move in any direction.

Her brazen charge surprised the German player. Meinart was accustomed to goalkeepers playing much more conservatively. She slowed and faked, but Scurry didn't take the bait. Meinart spun around and faked again, but Scurry still refused to be fooled.

Meinart's indecision cost her the advantage she had gained on the breakaway. She was stuck twenty-five yards short of the goal with Briana Scurry scowling in her face.

She finally got off a weak shot, trying to chip the ball over Scurry's head. But the American goalkeeper was ready. She emerged from her crouch and raced back, tracking the ball like a baseball outfielder. She caught the soft shot in both hands and hugged it close to her body.

On the American bench, Scurry's teammates jumped in the air and started shouting and clapping. The crowd roared. The save keyed an American surge, and the United States went on to win, 2–1. Scurry ended the game with six saves, including two from point-blank range.

After the game, the American coaches went out of their way to praise her play. "She still needs a lot of game experience," said Anson Dorrance, "but she played like a veteran. She was outstanding." The victory improved her record with the team to 5–1. "We're just trying to polish a diamond," added Dorrance.

Scurry was a little embarrassed by all the attention. "I'm just trying to get better," she said. "My biggest need is reading the game."

Scurry downplayed her save against Meinart. "When she broke through, I was surprised she didn't try to chip it over me earlier," she said. "I had to wait for her to make the first move, and I guess she got tired of me standing there. She didn't know what to do."

But the American coaches knew what to do. Briana Scurry was, without question, the first-string American goalkeeper. Sparked by her performance, the U.S. went on to win the Chiquita Cup, beating China, 1–0, and then overwhelming Norway, 4–1. Briana's play during the tournament had been so stellar that she was named tournament MVP. With Scurry in the goal, the United States looked like the odds-on favorite to win the upcoming World Cup.

After the tournament Coach DiCicco commented, "Although she is one of the younger and least experienced members of the team, she is supremely confident in goal and has earned the respect of her teammates. . . . She can become the greatest woman goalkeeper in the world. She'll be with us for quite a while, because her services are needed. With the World Cup around the corner and the Olympics in '96, I would say she could be here a long time."

That was fine with Scurry. "It seems like a long time ago when I first started playing soccer and they made me play goalkeeper," she said. "I'm at a different level now. Playing at this level is pressure-packed, but very exciting. I'm ecstatic at the thought of playing in the World Cup."

And with Briana Scurry in goal, so were her teammates.

"We did it!" Briana Scurry seems to say as she raises her arms in celebration next to teammate Carla Overbeck after the U.S. team won the gold medal in the 1996 Olympics.

Briana Scurry and Carin Gabarra circle the field with the American flag after winning the gold medal in the 1996 Olympics.

Briana Scurry is one hundred percent concentration during a practice
session before the 1999 Women's World Cup quarterfinals.

Briana Scurry celebrates with her teammates after beating Germany in the 1999 Women's World Cup quarterfinals.

Down but not out — Briana Scurry makes the save, with a little help from teammate Joy Fawcett, in the semifinals of the 1999 Women's World Cup against Brazil.

Briana Scurry denies Brazil a goal in the semifinals of the 1999 Women's World Cup.

On her way to a shutout, Briana Scurry nabs the ball in midair during a tense moment in the 1999 Women's World Cup semifinals.

Facing her toughest challenge, a kick during the shootout in the final game of the 1999 Women's World Cup, Scurry lunges . . .

...and makes the save that defeats China! The U.S. national team wins the Cup!

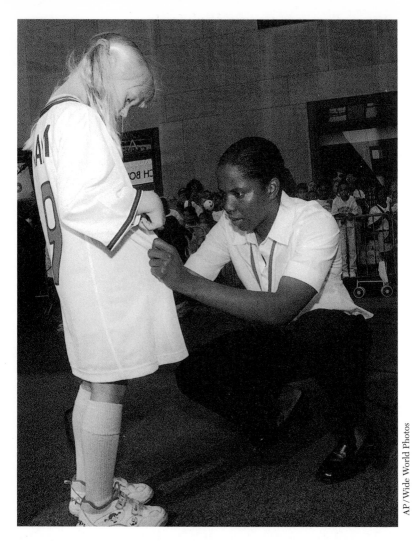

A hero to thousands, including this girl whose T-shirt she signs on the set of NBC's *Today Show*, Briana Scurry is the number one goalkeeper in the world.

Briana Scurry's Career Highlights

1989:
Voted top female athlete in Minnesota her senior year in high
  school
Selected as an All-American

1991:
Started all 19 games for UMass Minutewomen, allowing only 9
  goals and recording 12 shutouts

1992:
Started 13 games for UMass, recording 7 shutouts

1993:
Started all 23 games for UMass, recording 15 shutouts and a
  0.48 GAA, the third best in the country
Helped UMass reach the semifinals of the NCAA tournament
NCSAA Second-Team All-American, All-Northeast Region,
  and All–New England First Team selections
Won two national goalkeeper of the year awards

1994:
Debuted with national team on March 16, 1994, against
  Portugal
Recorded first shutout with national team on March 16, 1994,
  against Portugal
Named MVP of Chiquita Cup

1995:
Recorded most shutouts (9) in single year to date
Missed 1995 Women's World Cup due to back injury

(continued on next page)

1996:
Member of the Olympic gold medal team

1998:
Member of the Goodwill Games gold medal team

1999:
Member of the Women's World Cup champions

Briana Scurry's Statistics

Year	W—L—T	Games Played	Games Started	Minutes	Goals Against	Shutouts	Goals Against Average
1994	11—1—0	12	12	1080	5	7	0.42
1995	11—2—2	15	15	1344	11	9	0.74
1996	15—1—1	17	16	1495	11	8	0.66
1997	10—1—0	11	11	912	7	7	0.69
1998	15—1—2	19	17	1620	9	12	0.50
1999	16—2—0	18	18	1605	11	11	0.62
Totals	78—8—5	92	89	8056	54	54	0.61

Chapter Six:
1995

The Wrong Medal

Led by Scurry's steady and spectacular goalkeeping, the U.S. women's team easily qualified for the World Cup, winning their regional qualifier by beating Mexico, Trinidad and Tobago, Jamaica, and Canada by a combined score of 36–1. After the qualifying tournament the team broke up for several months to get some rest before resuming training.

While some team members traveled overseas to play with club teams, and others went back to work, Scurry returned to UMass to work toward her degree. At the same time she continued working out and staying in shape.

It was while Scurry was at UMass that she received the news that rocked her and the team to the core. Coach Anson Dorrance had decided to resign as national team coach to concentrate on his duties as coach of North Carolina. The rapid expansion of women's soccer had made it impossible for him to hold both positions. There was just too much to do. Both positions were full-time jobs.

Though saddened by Dorrance's decision, Scurry had reason to be happy as well, because assistant coach Tony DiCicco was picked to take over for Dorrance. Briana knew that DiCicco would make her job a little easier. Under Dorrance, the team had focused primarily on offense. That placed a lot of re-sponsibility on the goalkeeper to keep the other team from scoring.

But DiCicco had once been a goaltender for the U.S. men's team, and he was more concerned with defense than Dorrance had been. He instituted some subtle changes in the way the team played. "He's brought a new perspective on defense," Scurry said later. "Our forwards are playing more defen-sively. That can only help. None of our offense has been taken away."

The team got back together in January of 1995 to train in earnest for the World Cup. The women on the team were thrilled to be in camp and didn't take long to adapt to DiCicco's changes and to their new teammates. The transitions were made a bit easier because of where they were.

For the first time in history, the U.S. women's national team had their own training facility, built just for them by the USSF in Orlando, Florida. In the past, they had usually trained at colleges during school vacations, living in dorms and using athletic facilities at odd hours when they weren't in use by the schools. Many other national teams had had their own facilities for years.

Having their own facility gave the team several advantages. They had their own weight room and locker room as well as their own dormitory to stay in. Working together every day allowed them to grow closer as a team. That would be important entering the World Cup. They knew their ability to play together and get along would be crucial to their success.

Throughout the winter and spring the team alternated between spending several weeks training together and breaking camp to go on tour to publicize their sport by playing "friendlies" (games that are played for the sake of competition) against other teams from around the world. With the Olympics only a year away the team finally started getting some publicity. Briana did her part by appearing in a commercial for one of the team's sponsors, Nike. "I never expected this in a million years," she said when she was selected for the spot.

As the team prepared for the Cup, Scurry continued to solidify her position as number-one goalkeeper. Apart from a 2–0 loss to Denmark and a shoot-out loss to Norway, the United States was undefeated in 1995, ending the season with an 11–2–2 record. Scurry had been spectacular. During one stretch she played goal for an incredible 381 straight minutes without allowing a score.

Full of confidence, the team prepared to leave for Sweden to compete in the 1995 World Cup. Scurry hoped to avenge the only losses on her record, saying, "I'm definitely looking forward to playing them [Denmark and Norway]. I'd like to get a little piece of Norway." She felt that the U.S. team was the best in the world. "No one can beat this team when this team is on," she said. "It's scary. We can pretty much dismantle any team in the world when we're on. I don't know what other country can say that."

But despite her optimism, there was some cause for concern. Though she had a strong showing during the season, Scurry was still one of several new players on the team and some players were still making adjustments to her style. In addition, star Michelle Akers was sick with chronic fatigue syndrome. No one was certain how much she'd be able to play in the World Cup.

The Americans arrived in Sweden in late May and spent several days training together before the tournament opened on June 6. They faced a grueling schedule that called on them to play six games in thirteen days, but when the tournament started, they felt ready to take on all challengers to their World Cup title.

The U.S. played China in the opener. Although the Chinese were improving rapidly, few observers expected them to keep pace with the Americans. But only seven minutes into the game, Michelle Akers was involved in a collision, simultaneously hurting her knee and suffering a concussion. She was forced from the game.

Akers was an important player to the team. Not

only was she a dangerous scorer and a team veteran, she was one of the strongest defensive players in the world.

The team missed her leadership. For the rest of the game they played poorly on defense. They had several defensive breakdowns and didn't give Scurry much of a chance to make saves. The game ended in a 3–3 tie.

The United States was in a tough spot. In order to advance to the semifinals and have an opportunity to defend their title, the team had to finish either first or second in their group. That meant they absolutely had to win their second game against always-tough Denmark.

The U.S. came out fired-up and took a 2–0 lead. The U.S. dominated throughout. Then, with only a few minutes remaining in the game, Scurry gathered up a loose ball, bounced it several times, and punted it far downfield, just as she had done all game long.

Then the inexplicable happened. Referee Mamadouba Camara started blowing his whistle and waving his hand in the air. He ran up to Scurry and issued her a red card, ruling that she had handled the ball out of the penalty area.

Scurry was stunned. She thought she'd remained in the box. So did Coach DiCicco. He argued vehemently against the call, charging that the referee had misinterpreted the rule. At the most, he thought Scurry should have received a yellow card. Even the Danish coach later admitted that he disagreed with the call.

But the referee was adamant. Not only did Scurry have to leave the game, she was automatically suspended from the next game as well. Even worse, because the United States had already used up its three allotted substitutions, back-up goalkeeper Saskia Webber wasn't allowed to enter the game to replace Scurry. Coach DiCicco had to put one of the players already in the game into goal. In desperation he had Mia Hamm play goalkeeper.

Fortunately, Denmark failed to score in the final minutes even though they had a player advantage. Then in the last game of group play Webber filled in admirably for Scurry against Australia and the United States won, 4–1, to advance to the next round of play. Briana returned to the lineup and the U.S. beat Japan to advance to the semifinals and a rematch against Norway.

The Americans entered the game at less than one hundred percent. Michelle Akers returned to the lineup, but was slowed by a heavy knee brace. And forward Carin Gabarra, who'd been the MVP of the 1991 World Cup, was suffering from severe back spasms.

The injuries seriously hampered the American attack from the start. Then, only eleven minutes into the game, Norway was awarded a corner kick.

The kick was perfect, and Ann Aaroenes deftly headed it past Scurry into the net. As Briana later described the play, "That one ball just had eyes. It went straight for her head. That was a great ball, great serve."

Norway didn't back off. They continued to press play into the American end as the U.S. struggled to mount a counterattack. Scurry kept the game close by making some amazing saves, even earning praise from her opponents.

But the Americans just couldn't score. Norwegian

goalkeeper Bente Norbdy was just as spectacular as Scurry. In the end, the Norwegians won, 1–0. There would be no World Cup championship in 1995 for the American women.

At the end of the game they looked crestfallen as the ecstatic Norwegians celebrated their victory by doing a snake dance on the field. As the victors rejoiced, the Americans gathered together on the sidelines. They promised each other that they would never forget that moment. The next time, they promised, they would be the ones celebrating.

Despite the defeat, the team had to regroup and play again two days later in the consolation round, facing China to decide third place.

Even though it was a consolation game, Scurry didn't treat it that way. She played her best game of the tournament, turning the Chinese back again and again, leading Mia Hamm to say later, "Bri was unbelievable. She saved us." The U.S. won, 2–0. Then the team sat together in the stands and watched Norway win the Cup with a 2–0 win over Germany.

After the final the team took the field for the closing ceremonies of the tournament, to receive their bronze medals. Afterward they paraded around the field holding a sign that said WE'LL BE BACK.

The Olympics were only a year away. No one on the team was satisfied with a bronze medal. They had gold in mind.

Chapter Seven:
1996

Running Away with the Gold

When Scurry and her teammates returned to the United States everyone went her separate way. After so much intensive training and competition, they were exhausted and needed some time to relax and recuperate.

But as soon as her plane landed, Briana received some bad news. Her mother told her that her ten-year-old nephew Jerome, who was ill with leukemia, had been hospitalized with a serious infection. He'd nearly died while Briana was in Sweden. Scurry's family had kept his illness a secret because they didn't want to distract her.

She immediately went to the hospital to visit him. While she was there, she gave him her bronze medal.

That gesture was just one sign that Scurry was

growing up. She was beginning to realize that being a member of the national team meant she had a responsibility that went beyond soccer. "Soccer has deepened other parts of my life and given me a sense of responsibility," she has said. Spurred by her nephew's illness, Scurry became involved with the Make-A-Wish Foundation, which fulfills the dreams of ill children. When a friend of hers became sick with AIDS, she also began donating her time to various AIDS causes.

But shortly after her return to the United States, Scurry was nearly involved in a tragedy herself. She was in a car accident. Although she wasn't seriously hurt, she did injure both her shoulder and her back. After a period of rest, she knew she would have to work extra hard in order to get back in shape. She hoped she would be ready to play when the team got together at training camp in December of 1995 to prepare for the Olympics.

Fortunately, Scurry healed quickly. She spent the fall getting back in shape and serving as an assistant coach at the University of Arkansas. But she looked forward to resuming her place in the national team's starting lineup. Everyone on the team felt invigorated after the time off and could hardly wait to re-sume training.

But there was just one problem. Despite the gains women's soccer had made over the last few years, the United States women's team was still treated differently by the USSF than the men's team. In general, members of the women's team weren't paid as much or offered the same incentives as the men.

The USSF signed the members of the team to contracts that would pay them through the Olympics, but those contracts didn't pay the players until they got to camp. While some members of the team had coaching jobs or other sources of income, others didn't. They felt that they should have been paid for dedicating themselves to the team for much of the year for the 1995 World Cup.

The USSF also offered the players a $250,000 bonus if they won a gold medal at the Olympics. The players thought that was great, but the men's team was promised a bonus if they won any kind of medal. If the women failed to win the gold, they wouldn't get anything.

The veteran players on the team, including Michelle Akers, Julie Foudy, Mia Hamm, and Briana

Scurry, thought that was wrong. The players got together and decided not to attend camp until the issues were resolved.

Officials of the USSF were livid. They tried to pretend the team could get along without their best players and invited other women to try out for the team. But after several weeks it became clear that if the United States was to have any chance of winning a medal at the Olympics, they needed their best players. Finally, the USSF caved in to the players' demands.

When the team resumed training in January 1996, they were closer than ever. The dispute had drawn them together. They promised each other not to be satisfied with anything less than a gold medal.

Everyone worked harder than ever before, pushing one another in practice and in the weight room to get in the best condition of their lives. They all knew that the opportunity to play for a gold medal in the Olympics held in their own country was an unprecedented opportunity to publicize their sport. They didn't want to miss their chance.

After touring Brazil in January and emerging with four wins, the team returned to the United States and began an ambitious series of friendlies through-out the country against various international teams. Coach DiCicco had instituted some changes, switching several players between positions and increasing the team's focus on defense. The team's first big tests came in back-to-back games against Norway.

Although the United States split, defeating Norway, 3–2, and losing, 2–1, the team was relatively pleased with their performance. They had held Norway to only a handful of shots on goal. Although they were disappointed to lose, they were pleased with the way their new defense was coming together.

Over the next several months they played thirteen more friendlies, winning all thirteen by an aggregate score of 48–6! Scurry played almost every minute in goal and was spectacular, while Mia Hamm, Kristine Lilly, Michelle Akers, and Julie Foudy provided powerhouse offense.

In anticipation of the Olympics, several of the games were televised to increase recognition of the team. It worked. With each game, interest grew. At the beginning of their tour, only one or two thousand fans would turn out to see them play. By the end of the tour, the crowds had more than doubled.

Wherever they went, they were met by growing mobs of young soccer players, particularly girls who saw the team members as role models. Scurry and her teammates loved meeting their young fans. Briana, in particular, looked forward to showing young African-Americans that it was possible for them to play soccer despite the fact, as she said, that "there's not a lot of grass in the inner city." Whenever she met with young players, she explained to them that with hard work and determination, they could do anything they wished.

But neither Scurry nor her teammates were accustomed to all the attention. One morning Briana was awakened by a telephone call from a reporter for *Sports Illustrated.* While she was still groggy, he asked her how she would celebrate if the United States won the gold medal at the Olympics. "I'll run naked through the streets," she said, not thinking.

A few weeks later she was shocked when the story appeared and contained that quotation. Her teammates teased her mercilessly and the press kept asking her if she really planned to do what she said. Fortunately, Briana reacted with good humor.

She was thrilled to be in the Olympics. "I am absolutely living my dream," she told a reporter. "I grew up watching Mary Lou Retton and Carl Lewis perform such wonderful things. I remember how proud they looked representing their country. I can't wait to do the same thing."

The Olympic Games opened in Atlanta in late July. The soccer competition was arranged much like the World Cup, with the eight teams divided into two groups. The top two teams in each group would advance to the medal round. First-round play was held in a variety of locations. The Americans opened play on July 21, in Orlando, site of their training center, against Denmark.

When they took the field for their first game, they could hardly believe it. More than 20,000 fans greeted them with raucous cheers. It was the largest crowd to ever see a women's soccer match in the United States.

For the first thirty minutes of the game each team played conservatively. Neither wanted to give up the first goal. But in the thirty-fourth minute Denmark's Gitte Krogh got free on a breakaway.

Briana was ready. With an aggressive charge, she came out of the goal toward Krogh. Krogh rushed her shot. Scurry skipped to one side, bent, and smothered the ball for a save.

The play seemed to fire up the team. Two minutes later Tisha Venturini scored off a throw-in. The U.S. rolled to a 3–0 win.

The Americans powered through Sweden in their second game, winning 2–1 to clinch a spot in the semifinals. Scurry was almost perfect. Sweden's only score came on an own-goal when an American player inadvertently knocked the ball into the U.S. goal. Team USA then tied China, 0–0, as each team played conservatively to protect their place in the medal round.

Medal-round play took place in Athens, Georgia, in gigantic Sanford Stadium. The U.S. played Norway on July 28. The winner would play for the gold medal.

Nearly 70,000 fans greeted the team when they entered the stadium. Over the course of the Olympics interest in the team had grown. Now, with a world-wide television audience looking on, the team looked forward to making good on their promise to beat Norway and avenge their 1995 World Cup defeat.

Eighteen minutes into the game, the chances of that looked dim. Linda Medalen broke free and blasted the ball past Briana to give Norway a 1–0 lead.

Then the American defense stiffened, giving Norway virtually no opportunities to score. Meanwhile, the offense went on attack. But even though the Americans outshot Norway by more than three-to-one, with only fifteen minutes remaining in the game, the U.S. still trailed, 1–0.

Then a Norwegian player cut down Mia Hamm near the goal. The United States was awarded a penalty kick, which Michelle Akers blasted into the goal to tie the game.

Scurry remained firm in the American goal and the game entered overtime. The American defense continued to shut down Norway while the U.S. pressed their attack. Ten minutes into overtime Shannon MacMillan hammered home a goal to give the United States the win. With Norway behind them, the coveted gold medal was only one game away.

Interest in the final contest was high. Over the course of the Games the American public had discovered women's soccer and fallen in love with the sport and the U.S. team. Women's soccer is a slower and more strategic game than men's soccer, which gave American audiences relatively unfamiliar with the sport a chance to learn the game. Scurry and her teammates went out of their way to be accommodating of both the press and the fans, which many observers found refreshing. The women on the team weren't just great athletes; they were great people.

Sanford Stadium was packed to overflowing when the Americans came out on the field to warm up for the gold-medal game on August 1. The largest crowd ever to see a women's sporting event chanted, "USA! USA!" over and over. Thousands of fans waved flags as they cheered.

Briana went through her usual routine before the game. She listened to loud rock music, what she refers to as her "psych-up songs," to get pumped up before she took the field. But as game time approached she got more and more focused. In addition to the 76,481 people in the stands, millions if not billions more were watching on television around the world. But Briana wasn't nervous. This was the kind of pressure she liked.

"I have a little skill and a little knowledge. I am very fortunate to be where I am today," she told a reporter before the game. The way she figured it, she practiced every day against the best players in the world. "That's why I don't let things bother me in the game," she said. "The pressure they put on a goalkeeper in practice is great preparation. The game is actually easier."

Just before the game, Coach DiCicco had reminded his confident team that their opponent was a very good team and that he expected China to play very aggressively. Chinese forward Sun Wen was considered one of the best players in the world and goalkeeper Gao Hong's talents had earned her the nickname "The Great Wall of China." To win the gold medal, DiCicco cautioned, the Americans would have to play their best game of the Olympics.

At the beginning of the game Coach DiCicco's prediction of China's play proved accurate. The Chinese went on the attack immediately. Star forward Sun Wen got the ball in front of the U.S. goal several times, but each time she did, Scurry came charging out and turned her away.

Eighteen minutes into the game, the score was still 0–0. Then Mia Hamm took a cross pass from Kristine Lilly and sent a low, booming shot toward the Chinese goal. Gao Hong dove and blocked the shot off the post, but Shannon MacMillan gathered the rebound and put it into the open net to give the Americans a 1–0 lead.

Scurry tried to stay focused. She knew from experience that the most dangerous time for a goalkeeper is often right after her own team scores. The opposition usually goes on the attack while the scoring team suffers a letdown.

Sure enough, the Chinese took command of the game. Twelve minutes after MacMillan's goal, Wen caught the American defense napping and broke out from midfield with the ball. As U.S. captain Carla Overbeck tried to catch up and Brandi Chastain raced from the side to the goal line, Sun Wen moved toward the goal.

Scurry decided to come out and challenge her as she had before. This time, however, the Chinese forward anticipated Scurry's move. From twenty yards out she chipped the ball toward the goal. "I think she knew I was coming," Briana said later, "'cause I had been coming out and snuffing her other times."

Scurry jumped, but the shot went just over her fingers. Brandi Chastain sprinted across the goal and tried to block it, but couldn't do so. The game was tied, 1–1. "I came out too soon, too far," lamented Scurry later.

But she knew she couldn't let that goal disrupt her game. She had to retain her concentration for the rest of the match.

The game turned into a strategic, defensive struggle played out at midfield. Neither team managed to break through for the remainder of the half. But only fifteen minutes into the second half, Scurry was challenged again. China's Sun Qingmei broke open down the middle.

After being beaten by a lob shot, many goalkeepers would have turned tentative, stayed back, and played it safe, hoping for some help from their defense. But that wasn't the way Scurry played.

Once more she came out to challenge the shooter. Qingmei rushed her shot and Scurry dove sideways and was able to block it.

Scurry's teammates seemed energized after the save and pushed play into the Chinese end, attacking the goal repeatedly. Finally, with only twenty-two minutes left to play, Mia Hamm passed to Joy Fawcett. As Gao Hong turned to stop her, Fawcett made a perfect centering pass to Tiffeny Milbrett, who slipped the ball past Hong before she could react. The Americans led, 2–1.

China tried desperately to tie the score, but Scurry and her teammates were the best team in the world at maintaining a lead. A short time later, time ran out for the Chinese — and the Americans were officially the best team in the world, period.

The victorious U.S. team collapsed together in a huge knot of happiness. Some fans handed them an American flag and they began jogging around the field with it, waving to family and friends in the stands. Finally, they mounted a podium at midfield and, as the national anthem played, each woman received her gold medal.

The competition and medal ceremony were over,

but the celebration was just beginning. After the game, Scurry's teammates wouldn't allow her to forget the quote she had made to *Sports Illustrated* several months before. So, at 2:00 the next morning, as the team celebrated, Scurry and a friend drove to a very dark, quiet, and empty Athens side street. While her friend operated a video camera, Scurry took off her clothes and made a quick dash about twenty yards down the street and back, then jumped into the car.

When she returned to the team hotel, she played the tape for her teammates. As they laughed and roared, they watched a blurry image of Briana doing just as she had said, running through the streets of Athens naked, except for one thing — the gold medal that hung around her neck.

Chapter Eight:
1996-1998

Decisions, Decisions

After the Olympics, the members of the American team had some decisions to make. It would be three long years until the next Women's World Cup, and four years to the next Olympics. That was a long time between major competitions. Coach DiCicco said later, "A lot of players questioned whether they wanted to do this for another four years." He wanted to make sure everyone on the team was really committed to playing. The team broke up for a while to give the women some time to figure out what they wanted to do next.

Scurry was exhausted. All she planned to do was "regenerate and heal," she told the press. She explained, "I've gotten myself so stressed out the last seven months. All I want to do right now is sleep in and eat bad food." That's exactly what she did.

Although Briana rejoined her teammates when they resumed training for the 1997 season, she was a little distracted. Like many of her teammates, she wasn't sure if she wanted to put her life on hold for another three or four years. After all, she had a college degree and was still entertaining the idea of going to law school or starting a business, telling one reporter that she wanted to be financially independent by the time she was thirty years old. Though the bonus she had received after winning the gold medal helped her toward that goal, there was no guarantee that she'd be able to reach it while playing on the national women's soccer team.

She was also thinking about playing other sports. It was hard to sustain a soccer career. There was no professional league in the United States. The only places women were paid to play soccer were Japan and a few European countries. Scurry didn't want to leave the United States. She played a little club soccer to stay in shape, but after playing at the international level, club soccer wasn't very challenging.

She also missed playing basketball. Since she'd last played organized basketball in high school, women's basketball had become extremely popular. There were even two professional leagues, the Women's National Basketball Association (WNBA) and the American Basketball League (ABL). Scurry toyed with the idea of starting to play basketball again and trying out for a professional team.

Although she played well with the U.S. team in 1997, Coach DiCicco sensed that Scurry wasn't quite as committed and enthusiastic as she'd been during the Olympics. In December of 1997, when the team traveled to Brazil for a short tour, DiCicco left Scurry behind. He recalled later, "I told her to sort it out, to decide if soccer was in her future."

Scurry wasn't really upset at being left behind; she understood, admitting later that after the Olympics, "It was kind of an anticlimactic depression thing for a few months. I was like, okay, now what?" While the team was in Brazil, she thought about her future.

While Tracy Ducar and Jen Mead filled in for Scurry, the United States played the rapidly improving Brazil team in four games. In the first three games, Brazil took a lead before the Americans staged comebacks to win. But in the final game

Brazil beat the U.S., 1–0, their first victory over the United States. "Now they know it can be done," said Coach DiCicco. "And that's dangerous for the future."

In January 1998, Briana rejoined the team at training camp. While they were in Brazil, she realized how much she missed playing with them and being part of the team. Besides, the chance to compete in the World Cup to be played in the United States in 1999 was a once-in-a-lifetime opportunity. At the Olympics, Scurry and her teammates had made the American public aware of women's soccer. In the World Cup, they hoped to make them fans. When they had been growing up, there were few women athletes to serve as role models. They hoped to fulfill that role for the next generation of young athletes.

Scurry rededicated herself to soccer. Like everyone else on the team, she knew she would have to play well to keep her place. Coach DiCicco wouldn't hesitate to replace her or anyone else if he felt it would help the team.

Scurry traveled with the team to China for the Guangzhou Tournament in late January. Any doubts her teammates had about her dedication to the sport vanished during that tournament. Scurry collected three straight shutouts, including her first in eight tries against Norway, as the United States won the competition. "To get three shutouts against teams of this caliber is something that hasn't happened in a long time," said team cocaptain Carla Overbeck.

Over the next few months, although DiCicco occasionally experimented with either Tracy Ducar or Saskia Webber in the goal, Scurry resumed her place as the team's number-one goalkeeper. The team played in a number of friendlies, then captured titles in both the Goodwill Games and the U.S. Women's Cup. Briana was almost perfect. After Scurry rejoined the team, the U.S. racked up an amazing 15–1–2 record in the games in which she played. Scurry gave up only nine goals and notched twelve shutouts, as the Americans had their most successful season ever.

Her stellar play didn't go unnoticed. Coach DiCicco told one reporter that "the modern game requires more from a goalkeeper, and she has increased her range because she has the athleticism to do it. . . . Someday all keepers will play like her." Her teammates put it more simply. They just called her "the best goalkeeper in the world."

In the 1999 World Cup, Scurry would have an opportunity to prove she was just that.

Chapter Nine:
1999

The Way to the World Cup

For the American team, there was more at stake in the 1999 World Cup than just holding on to the world championship. The event would be the culmination of years of effort by team members to promote their sport. In some ways, the future of the sport in the U.S. depended upon their success.

The team believed that if they could just get fans to watch them play, the public would learn to enjoy the sport. If that happened they knew the future of women's soccer in the U.S. and all over the world would be secure. Only a few years earlier they had played and practiced in obscurity. Talk of professional leagues and television coverage for their sport sounded absurd. But through hard work and determination those dreams didn't seem so remote anymore.

Scurry and her teammates took their responsibilities as ambassadors for the game seriously. They knew that young soccer players looked up to them as role models. Briana appreciated in particular how important she was to African-American children, saying, "I definitely see myself as a role model for African-American kids, all kids." African-American girls see few African-American female athletes. Briana said, "When they see me out there, [I hope] they see something they can aspire to. . . . I take very seriously my role of showing African-American youth, and people in general, that we can excel in sport — or in anything."

To prepare for the World Cup the team spent several weeks at the start of 1999 at training camp in Florida. Then they embarked on an ambitious schedule of friendlies and tournaments to get ready to play and help promote their sport. As they toured the country, crowds slowly built. Several games were televised nationally, and throngs of young soccer players greeted the team everywhere. Everyone, it seemed, was getting excited about the World Cup.

Expectations for the team were tremendous. Everyone counted on them to win the Cup; nothing less would do. Scurry and her teammates were under a great deal of pressure.

Although they played well in the months before the Cup, they weren't quite as dominant as they had been in 1998. Every team in the world was hoping to knock off the United States and every team in the world was improving rapidly.

In February they played the FIFA All-Stars, a team made up of the best players from the best teams in the world. Even though the FIFA squad had barely practiced together, they beat the Americans, 2–1, the team's first loss on American soil in forty-six games. Now the rest of the world knew the U.S. could be defeated.

In March, the team traveled to Portugal for the Algarve Cup, their last competition before the World Cup. The team hoped to win the tournament and convince the rest of the world they were still the team to beat in the World Cup.

But all of a sudden, the Americans were out of sync. In the opening game, they tied Sweden. After beating Finland, 4–0, they faced Norway in the semifinals.

Only eleven minutes into the contest Norway

tried a corner kick. The American defense cleared the cross but failed to cover the ball. Scurry was screened by the traffic in front of the goal and Norway blasted the shot home to go ahead, 1–0.

The Americans scrambled to catch up and managed to escape with a 2–1 win, but their confidence was shaken. In the tournament final against China they were beaten in every facet of the game and lost, 2–1. Scurry hadn't given up two goals in a game in months.

Although the team rebounded to beat China in a rematch in April, the Chinese came back to beat the Americans again in a third game, 2–1. All of a sudden, some observers were picking China to win the Cup.

The Americans' problems were both consistency and concentration. After dominating play for long periods of time they'd suffer a breakdown, particularly on defense. Not even Briana could stop every shot.

In the past the Americans' athletic ability had been enough to simply overwhelm most teams. But it appeared that their opponents had figured this out and increased their own training. In short, the competition was getting better.

Fortunately, there was still some time for the team to regroup. When they returned to the United States, they were able to regain their confidence against lesser competition. But once the World Cup began, they wouldn't have that luxury. Every team they would face had the potential to defeat them. Briana and her teammates had to be ready.

In the last few weeks before the start of the World Cup on June 19, interest in the competition continued to build. Members of the American team were becoming celebrities, appearing in television commercials promoting the Cup and making all sorts of public appearances. Even games that didn't include the American team were selling out; eventually more than a half million tickets were sold. On the precipice of the World Cup, the team sensed that they had an opportunity to help take their sport to the next level.

Their preparation was over. It was time to play. Now all they had to do was win.

Chapter Ten:
1999

Making the Save

The United States began group play on June 19, 1999, against Denmark at the Meadowlands football stadium in New Jersey. Nearly 80,000 fans greeted the team when they took the field.

Although the United States had recently dominated the Danish team, the Danes were still dangerous. In group play, a single loss can be devastating to a team. The Americans suspected the Danes would try to score an early goal, then stack their defense to keep the U.S. from scoring.

That put a lot of pressure on Briana. But she wasn't nervous. She looked forward to the game. She wanted to show the world that she was the best goalkeeper on the planet.

Just as the Americans expected, Denmark rushed

out at the beginning of the game and tried to steal an early lead. Only two minutes into the game they got a shot on goal, but it went wide of the left post. A few minutes later Briana made a great stop on a header off a corner kick.

The United States responded to Scurry's great save by launching an attack. Brandi Chastain fed the ball to Mia Hamm on the right side, who slammed it into the goal with her left foot to give the United States a 1–0 lead.

But Denmark didn't give up. They kept trying to press their attack. Just before halftime the Danes were awarded a free kick. Fortunately for the U.S., it went wide.

In the second half the American defense finally took command, giving Denmark few chances to score. Late in the game Julie Foudy and Kristine Lilly both scored, and the U.S. won, 3–0.

After the game Briana was full of praise for her teammates' offensive and defensive efforts, saying, "When my team is down in the other end, I love it. It's fine with me if we're dominating. . . . It's difficult at times when the other team gets a breakthrough, but I'm trained to handle the tough shots when they come at me. The more bored I am, the better."

The team traveled across the country to Chicago to play their next game, against Nigeria. They knew little about the Nigerian team apart from the fact that they played aggressively and were very quick.

The Nigerians proved that from the first moment of the game. They went on an all-out attack that threatened to overwhelm the Americans.

American midfielder Julie Foudy tried to head the ball out of the American goal box, but she mis-played the ball right to Nigeria's best player, "Marvelous" Mercy Akide. Scurry had no choice but to react to the ball, but Akide wisely passed it across the goal to an onrushing teammate, who fired it into the net before Scurry could recover. Nigeria led, 1–0, before the game was even two minutes old.

Scurry shouted encouragement to her teammates as she booted the ball downfield, but as soon as Nigeria got the ball back they came charging down into the American end again. With the ball free in front of the American goal, two U.S. defenders collided.

Scurry had to act quickly. She charged in front of the goal line to challenge for the ball. As she did, teammate Brandi Chastain smartly stepped in behind to help cover the net.

Scurry's charge forced Nigeria to rush the shot and Chastain guided the ball past the post and over the end line.

The save seemed to frustrate Nigeria, and the Americans soon regained their composure. Nigeria kept taking bigger and bigger chances on offense, and the Americans soon took command, scoring three times in only three minutes of play. The United States then closed with a rush to win, 7–1.

The victory virtually assured the U.S. a spot in the quarterfinals. For their final game in group play against North Korea, Coach DiCicco decided to rest some key players.

But he kept Scurry in the lineup. He wanted to make sure she stayed sharp. She did just that as the Americans came back after a scoreless first half to win, 3–1.

The victory clinched a place in the quarterfinals for the American team opposite Germany. Cup organizers had expected to sell only about 40,000 seats for the game, but interest was so high they had to print more tickets. Even President Clinton decided to attend.

Although some observers had picked the Germans to win the Cup, they had been a disappointment thus far. Still, like the Americans, they'd advanced to the quarterfinals despite not playing up to their potential.

For the third time in four games the Americans got off to a slow start, as Germany took control early and forced play. After one offensive thrust by the Germans, Brandi Chastain got control of the ball just in front of the U.S. goal.

She decided to pass the ball back to Scurry, a routine play. But Scurry expected Chastain to pass the ball back toward the sideline and broke in that direction. As she did, Chastain passed the ball to the middle.

Briana was going one way and the ball was going the other. She watched helplessly as it rolled over the goal line. The own-goal gave Germany an early 1–0 lead. That was dangerous. The Germans were talented enough to make a one-goal lead stand up.

But Scurry's teammates battled back to tie the

game, then slowly seemed to take control. Then, just before halftime, the Americans made a rare mistake.

The defense relaxed and Germany's Bettina Wiegmann got the ball at the top-right corner of the penalty area. She blasted a perfect shot with her left foot. Scurry dove, but it found the side of the net inside the far post. The Americans trailed, 2–1.

The team was stunned. At halftime Coach Di-Cicco told them they'd have to play their best in the second half or else their dream of winning the Cup would come to a premature end.

The Americans came out in the second half determined to keep that dream alive. Only four minutes into the half Brandi Chastain made up for her earlier mistake by scoring on a sliding shot after a corner kick, to tie the game.

The Americans took control. At the sixty-five-minute mark Shannon MacMillan entered the game and made a perfect corner kick, which Joy Fawcett headed into the goal. Finally, the United States was in front, 3–2. Nursing the lead, the Americans turned defensive for the rest of the game and escaped with a win.

Now only four teams remained in the competition. In the semifinals, China played Norway, while the United States faced Brazil.

The Americans knew that Brazil was a dangerous team. Soccer is the national sport in Brazil, and their team was both athletic and experienced. They were particularly talented on offense and were probably the most improved team in the tournament. Many observers predicted an upset.

Scurry and her teammates refused to let that happen. Since the game was being played on July 4, they had extra motivation. Briana had another reason for wanting to play her best. Her parents were in the crowd; it was the first World Cup game they'd been able to attend.

For once, the Americans jumped out to a quick lead. Only five minutes into the game, Julie Foudy shot the ball toward the goal from the left side. Brazilian goalkeeper Malvihna (Brazilian soccer players are traditionally referred to by one name) got her hands on the ball, but she failed to hold on. It bounced free and Cindy Parlow headed it into the open net for a 1–0 lead.

The Americans controlled play for much of the

first half, but then the Brazilians began to hit stride. All of a sudden they were beating the Americans to the ball. In the closing minutes of the first half, Scurry had to make two fine stops to preserve the lead.

But in the second half Brazil picked up right where they had left off. Just one minute into the second half, Brazilian star Nene shot a cannon toward the American goal from thirty-five yards out.

Often, such long-range shots can surprise the goalkeeper. But Scurry was ready. With the fast, twisting shot coming her way, she took a few quick steps back then jumped as high as she could. Arm outstretched, she punched at the ball with her hand and deflected it up. It hit the crossbar and sailed over the goal!

Ten minutes later, Nene worked free again. This time she was only twelve yards out when she sent a rocket toward the left corner, but once more Scurry read her perfectly and launched herself into the air just as Nene made her kick. She got her hands on the ball and knocked it wide. The Americans still led, 1–0!

Scurry's spectacular play left the Brazilians frustrated. They were outplaying the United States, yet they still trailed. As time began to run out, they became desperate.

Ten minutes before the end of the game Mia Hamm was fouled. Michelle Akers nailed the penalty kick to put the Americans ahead by two goals.

With Briana in the net, a two-goal lead with only ten minutes to play seemed like a twenty-goal margin. Brazil was unable to mount a serious threat and the United States won, 2–0. When the final whistle blew, Briana's teammates sprinted toward the American goal and crowded around her. They were going to the finals! They knew that she was the reason they had won the game.

After the game they gave her full credit for the win. They knew that if she hadn't played as well as she had, they would have lost.

"Thank God Bri is on our team," said Mia Hamm. "She was awesome today. Bri showed she is one of the best goalkeepers in the world."

Coach DiCicco agreed. "The number-one star for us today," were his words. Even the Brazilian coach called her "the great player of the game."

Scurry was gratified to have played so well at such

a critical time. "I feel awesome," she said. "The ball seemed big to me today. Any game where I can do my part and get my team in the final of the Women's World Cup is my best game. . . . I definitely think today was my best effort in my five years playing on the team." She gave some of the credit to the crowd. "The fans definitely made a difference for me, especially two in particular, my parents. . . . It's great to see the outpour of people supporting us."

She only hoped she could play as well in the final.

Chapter Eleven:
1999

Shoot-Out!

China defeated Norway by the stunning score of 5–0 to advance to the final against the Americans. Soccer experts from around the world thought the Chinese team was playing better than the Americans and had a good chance to win.

Both teams had a week off before the final. Scurry and her teammates used the time to get some rest and prepare for the game.

China posed some unique problems for the Americans. They played a very similar style, trying to dominate the game at midfield and then go on attack. Star forward Sun Wen was leading all scorers in the Cup and Gao Hong had given up the fewest goals.

Many people expected the game to be decided by the goalkeepers. Sun Wen even did a little trash-talking, telling a reporter, "We will bombard Scurry with all kind of shots. She had better be prepared."

Briana responded at a press conference. "Do I have to play great? I don't know. I know I have to do my job and not get caught up in the hype."

As game time neared, interest in the final increased. Organizers sold more than 90,000 tickets for the game at the Rose Bowl in Pasadena, California. The entire country had World Cup fever. Scurry and her teammates didn't want to let their fans down.

The day of the game dawned bright and clear. By the time the team took the field on the afternoon of July 10, the temperature was over ninety degrees. The stands were full of people, most of them wearing red, white, and blue. The president was in attendance again and the game was being broadcast all over the world. No women's sporting event had been seen by so many people, either in person or on television.

Briana tried to stay focused and not let the crowd distract her. She knew that if she lost her concentration against the Chinese for only a few seconds, it could cost the Americans the game.

When the game started the Americans played aggressively, beating the Chinese to the ball and not allowing them to penetrate past midfield. Scurry hoped her teammates could keep it up the whole game.

But the Chinese soon began to adjust. They deflected the American attack and the game started to be played almost entirely at midfield. Neither team had much of an opportunity to score.

But in the thirty-fourth minute, American defender Kate Sobrero fouled Pu Wei and the referee awarded China a free kick. The dangerous Sun Wen lined up to take China's first shot of the game.

She tried to drill the shot to a place in the goal where Briana couldn't get it, but she missed, sending it just over the top of the net. Scurry and her teammates breathed a collective sigh of relief.

Five minutes later Pu Wei got another chance, but her shot sailed wide. At halftime the game was scoreless.

Both teams came out in the second half determined

to not make mistakes. Although the U.S. put more pressure on the goal than China, they just couldn't get a shot past Gao Hong.

Late in the game, the Chinese started having more success. They received a corner kick and the ball sailed across the goalmouth. Scurry fought her way through a crowd toward the ball.

So did Michelle Akers and several Chinese players. Everyone went up for the ball at the same time. Akers got sandwiched between Scurry and a Chinese player. She fell to the ground.

Fortunately, the Americans were able to clear the ball, but Akers was both exhausted and hurt. She'd hit her head and suffered a concussion. On top of that, she was dehydrated. As she lay on the ground, the final whistle blew. A stretcher took her from the field.

Akers wasn't the only one who was feeling the temperature and the pressure. After ninety scoreless minutes, the heat and humidity had taken a toll on everyone. Players on both teams slumped to the ground, exhausted. But the game wasn't over yet. There was a fifteen-minute overtime to be played.

The team that scored first, making a so-called "golden goal," would win the game.

After a few minutes the overtime period got under way. Akers's absence seemed to fire up the Chinese. They suddenly seemed unaffected by the heat and began to play with more confidence. The Americans looked like the tired team.

China was awarded another corner kick. As the ball arched toward the goal, Scurry came out to get it. But a Chinese player beat her to it and went up to head the ball. The header shot past Scurry toward the far post.

In a corner kick situation, every player has a certain role. The far post was Kristine Lilly's responsibility.

She was right where she was supposed to be. She headed the ball out and Brandi Chastain cleared it. China had missed a golden opportunity to win. "Lil is a workhorse," Scurry said later. "There's no one I would trust more on the post."

The save seemed to wake up the Americans, and they took command. But the first overtime period ended without a score. After a brief break, the two teams went back out to play a second fifteen-minute overtime period.

As the clock ticked down, the Americans got several good shots off but weren't able to find the net. Finally, the whistle blew ending the second overtime. After 120 minutes of hard-fought soccer, the World Cup would be decided on penalty kicks!

In the penalty round each team alternates taking five shots on goal from twelve yards out. Whichever team scores the most goals wins.

Since first joining the national team, Briana had been in a shoot-out situation only once before, in a loss to Norway. But the team worked on penalty kicks nearly every day in practice. She had confidence in her own ability to block shots and in her teammates' to make theirs. "I knew I just had to make one [save] and my teammates would make their shots," she said later.

"It's all mental," she once explained to a reporter about the shoot-out. "The pressure's on the shooter."

Coach DiCicco gathered the team together before the shoot-out. He told Scurry to stay positive and strong. She nodded her head. She was so focused she could hardly speak.

She stood before her goal and Gao Hong stood before the other. The Chinese shooters gathered before Scurry and the Americans before Hong. The Chinese would shoot first.

Xie Huilin placed the ball on the ground and backed up. Then she stepped quickly toward it and drilled the shot to the left side.

Scurry broke for the ball. She couldn't reach it and the shot rifled into the net. The score was 1–0.

Now it was the Americans' turn. Scurry got up and turned around, her back to the field. She refused to look at her teammates as they took their shots, explaining later, "I used to [watch] with my club team, but it seemed like every time I did, they missed." The crowd would let her know if her teammates scored.

A few moments later she heard a loud roar. Carla Overbeck had just beaten Hong!

Now Qui Haiyan stepped in for China. She calmly blasted a shot into the left corner. China led, 2–1.

Once more Briana turned her back to the field. Once more she heard the crowd roar, as Joy Fawcett made her shot.

Now China's Liu Ying approached the ball. As she did, Scurry got a funny feeling.

"I had a feeling I could get that one as she was walking up," she remembered later. "Sometimes I get those feelings. I can't explain it. . . . It didn't look like she wanted to shoot it. She didn't have the confidence. You could see it the way she walked up there."

Scurry knew this would be her chance to stop the Chinese. As Ying approached the ball and swung her leg back to kick, Scurry pounced.

In a shoot-out the goalkeeper isn't supposed to move before the ball is struck, but they often do. It is up to the referee to call the infraction. If he does the player gets to shoot again.

Briana took a quick step forward, cutting down the angle, and then dove to her left just as Ying struck the ball. At the apex of her dive, the ball hit her hands and went wide.

YES! Briana jumped up, pumped her fists in the air, and yelled, "Come on! Come on!" exhorting the screaming crowd to cheer even louder. The fans roared in response and her teammates raised their arms in celebration.

Then Scurry turned her back on the field again.

Kristine Lilly made her shot to put the United States ahead, 3–2.

The next two Chinese players scored, as did America's Mia Hamm. The score was tied, 4–4. Brandi Chastain, America's fifth and final shooter, approached the ball. If she scored, the Americans would win the World Cup.

Briana turned her back to the field again. She didn't see Chastain kick the ball, and she didn't see her whip off her shirt and collapse to her knees, and she didn't see her teammates rush onto the field.

But she heard the roar of the fans and smiled. The U.S. had won the World Cup!

Briana ran from the field over to where her parents, her brother, and her friends were standing in the crowd cheering like everyone else. She gave them all a hug and stayed there for a while watching her teammates celebrate before she finally went down and joined them. When she did, she was greeted like a hero.

"Scurry has had such a wonderful tournament," Coach DiCicco said after the game. "She is the hero."

Briana Scurry hardly knew what to say. "It's my greatest moment on a soccer field. This is all so unbelievable," she said a few days later. "I'm still on cloud nine."

And with Briana Scurry in the goal, so is the American women's soccer team.

Matt Christopher

Sports Bio Bookshelf

Terrell Davis	Tara Lipinski
John Elway	Mark McGwire
Julie Foudy	Greg Maddux
Wayne Gretzky	Hakeem Olajuwon
Ken Griffey Jr.	Briana Scurry
Mia Hamm	Emmitt Smith
Grant Hill	Sammy Sosa
Derek Jeter	Mo Vaughn
Randy Johnson	Tiger Woods
Michael Jordan	Steve Young
Lisa Leslie	

The #1 Sports Series for Kids

Read them all!

All available in paperback from Little, Brown and Company